Pebble®

My World

Countries
in My World

by Ella Cane

Consulting Editor: Gail Saunders-Smith, PhD

CAPSTONE PRESS
a capstone imprint

Pebble Books are published by Capstone Press,
1710 Roe Crest Drive, North Mankato, Minnesota 56003
www.capstonepub.com

Library of Congress Cataloging-in-Publication Data
Cane, Ella.
Countries in my world / by Ella Cane.
pages cm. — (Pebble books. My world)
Includes index.
ISBN 978-1-4765-3122-9 (library binding)
ISBN 978-1-4765-3464-0 (paperback)
ISBN 978-1-4765-3470-1 (ebook pdf)
1. Geography—Juvenile literature. I. Title.
G133.C24 2014
910—dc23   2013005990

Summary: Simple text and full-color photographs introduce countries to
the reader.

Note to Parents and Teachers

The My World set supports national curriculum standards for
social studies related to people, places, and environments. This
book describes and illustrates countries. The images support
early readers in understanding the text. The repetition of words
and phrases helps early readers learn new words. This book
also introduces early readers to subject-specific vocabulary
words, which are defined in the Glossary section. Early readers
may need assistance to read some words and to use the Table
of Contents, Glossary, Read More, Internet Sites, and Index
sections of the book.

Printed in the United States   5469

Table of Contents

United States

What Is a Country?

A country is a piece
of land with borders.
But it's more than that.
Let's take a look at
some countries.

Government

Each country has
a government.
In the United States,
people elect a president
as leader.

Language

Many countries have
an official language.
Canada has two.
They are French
and English.

Money

Most countries have an official currency. In the United States, it's the U.S. Dollar.

Shanghai, China

People

The world has more than 7 billion people. China is the country with the most people. There are 1.3 billion people in China.

Siberia, Russia

14

Size

China may have people, but Russia has space. Russia is the country with the most land area.

Landforms

The land in any country is marked with landforms. Mount Everest is part of the countries of China and Nepal.

Some landforms cover several countries. The Sahara desert stretches across countries in northern Africa.

Number of Countries

The world has about 195 countries. This number changes as countries change. What do you know about your country?

Glossary

area—the total surface within a set of borders

border—the dividing line between two places

currency—the type of money a country uses

elect—to choose someone as a leader
by voting

government—the group of people who make
laws, rules, and decisions for a city, country
or state

landform—a natural feature of the land

language—the way people speak or talk

official—having the approval of a country
or certain group

Read More

Hirsch, Rebecca. *North America.* Rookie Read-About Geography. New York: Children's Press, 2012.

Hutmacher, Kimberly M. *Mountains.* Natural Wonders. Mankato, Minn.: Capstone Press, 2011.

Roop, Peter, and Connie. *China.* A Visit to. Chicago: Heinemann Library, 2008.

Internet Sites

FactHound offers a safe, fun way to find Internet sites related to this book. All of the sites on FactHound have been researched by our staff.

Here's all you do:

Visit *www.facthound.com*

Type in this code: 9781476531229

Check out projects, games and lots more at
www.capstonekids.com

Index

Word Count: 154
Grade: 1
Early-Intervention Level: 17

Editorial Credits
Shelly Lyons, editor; Juliette Peters, designer; Marcie Spence, media researcher;
Eric Manske, production specialist

Photo Credits
Capstone Studios: Karon Dubke, 10; Shutterstock: _EG_, 14, Alexander Raths, 20
(bottom), Arsgera, 16, Christopher Halloran, 6, Eniko Balogh, 18, FER737NG, 8,
Intrepix, cover, Kotomiti Okuma, 1, TonyV3112, 12, Vitoriano Junior, 4, 20 (top)